DEDICA

IN LOVING MEMORY OF MY MOTHER,

PATRICIA PATTERSON MCKENZIE

(I AM THANKFUL SHE GAVE ME THE SELF-CONFIDENCE

AND DETERMINATION TO BE DIFFERENT),

AND TWO FRIENDS,

MARIE CLAIRE FONTAINE AND FRANCES CURRIE KOBOS.

THEY ALL LIVED WITH GREAT PASSION

AND DIED WITH GREAT COURAGE.

TABLE OF CONTENTS

CONTENTS

DREAMS

Your DREAMS are the foundations of your successes. They will set you apart from the commonplace . . . but only if you follow them.

It has been said that if the DREAM is big enough, the facts don't count! That means that whatever the odds, you can overcome any obstacle if you are determined to make your DREAMS come true.

GOD DIDN'T MAKE US TO BE FAILURES OR FOOLS.

God made us for greatness;

our dreams are his tools.

CELINE

TAKE DELIGHT IN THE LORD, AND HE WILL GIVE YOU

COMMIT EVERYTHING YOU DO TO THE LORD.

I, _____,

FOLLOW MY DREAMS . . .

NOT MY PEERS.

YOUR HEART'S DESIRES.

TRUST HIM, AND HE WILL HELP YOU.

Psalm 37:4-5

4

Everything great begins with a dream and often with a dream that seems to defy reality. You have heard thrilling accounts of physically challenged people becoming world-class athletes, of impoverished children growing up to become captains of industry, of the modest beginnings of leaders in every field. All kinds of great accomplishments have sprung from the most humble roots. It is true that, with God's help, you can become anything you have the faith to become. God deals in big dreams, so dream big dreams!

What a joy to learn that life can be a quest, not a drudge! A mission that can be lived with an attitude of adventure and a sense of purpose.

God did not create you in his own image—and then send his Son to die for you—so that you could live a mediocre, meaningless, boring life. No! He has great plans for <u>you.</u>

He has put dreams in your heart that are yours and only yours. They are as individually yours as your fingerprints or your DNA.

So, believe in God, believe in yourself, and believe in the power of your dreams.

> SET YOUR SIGHTS
> ON THE DREAM AND
> NEVER GIVE UP.

JOY

JOY IS THE GREATEST SOURCE OF STRENGTH.
JOY COMES FROM KNOWING THAT GOD LOVES
YOU, KNOWING THAT YOU LOVE GOD, AND
KNOWING WHERE YOU ARE GOING TOGETHER.
JOY IS THE CURRENCY OF HEAVEN,
AVAILABLE ON EARTH ONLY TO THOSE WHO
TRULY TRUST IN GOD.

IN GOD WE TRUST

UNITED STATES CURRENCY

THE JOY OF THE LORD

I, _____,

WILL TRUST GOD IN ALL THINGS

. . . AND REJOICE!

IS YOUR STRENGTH!

Nehemiah 8:10

10

Happiness depends on what is happening around you, but joy is a supernatural gift from God. The joy of the Lord can overcome all circumstances as long as you trust your Creator. This very trust is what enabled Christian martyrs to sing joyful hymns as they were tortured and killed for their faith.

In 1995, my friend and classmate Frances "Bebe" Currie Kobos (to whose memory this book is dedicated) was trapped in a tragic catastrophe—a huge pileup of trucks and automobiles on a long bay bridge in Alabama. Dozens of vehicles were involved in the massive accident caused by the early morning fog.

The flames from a burning truck encroached steadily, as a rescue worker did everything in his power to free Bebe from the wreckage. Finally, extreme heat forced him to give up. "I'm so sorry, I'm so sorry," he sobbed, backing away. And Bebe, left alone in her burning automobile, had the compassion to forgive that worker as he retreated.

The last sight of Bebe was life changing for those who were there and for those who heard the story of what happened. Flames were licking over her shoulder, a bystander said, but somehow she was peaceful. Bebe died reciting Psalm 23. She had known the joy of the Lord for a long time, and it was with her until the very end of this life, truly overcoming all circumstances. The very same joy is available for anyone who trusts God.

THAT IS HIS PROMISE,
AND HE IS FAITHFUL.

OPTIMISM

LOOKING FOR THE BRIGHT SIDE OF THINGS WILL OFTEN BRING THE POSITIVE SIDE OF THINGS RIGHT TO YOUR DOOR. THAT'S THE POWER OF OPTIMISM!

14

KEEP YOUR FACE
TO THE SUNSHINE

and you cannot see the shadow.

HELEN KELLER,
blind and deaf American essayist

FIX YOUR THOUGHTS ON WHAT IS TRUE AND HONORABLE
ARE PURE AND LOVELY AND ADMIRABLE. THINK ABOUT THINGS
AND WORTHY OF PRAISE. . . . AND THE GOD OF

I, _____,

TRUST GOD TO BRING GOOD FROM

EVERY SITUATION THAT I

COMMIT TO HIM.

AND RIGHT. THINK ABOUT THINGS THAT

THAT ARE EXCELLENT

PEACE WILL BE WITH YOU.

Philippians 4:8-9

16

Life is sometimes hard, and even though God's will is only for the best, we live in an imperfect (no kidding!) world. The hard times are the times to remember that God can cause all things to work together for good for those who love him (Romans 8:28). Jesus tells us that he will never leave us or forsake us. He also says that although in this world there will be trouble, we should be of good cheer, because he has overcome the world.

The book, <u>The Diary of a Young Girl,</u> is a treasure of optimism in the face of the most evil circumstances imaginable. It was written by Anne Frank, a lovely young teenager, who looked for the best while she was hidden in an attic for months deprived of freedom, privacy, even food. She lived with the moment-to-moment fear of being discovered, dragged away, and executed by the Nazis (which is exactly what happened shortly before her sixteenth birthday). In the midst of her trials, Anne Frank kept a diary that has inspired and encouraged millions of readers to have faith and courage and optimism in times of great hardship. Even in her darkest hours, she was able to say in her diary, "Whoever is happy will make others happy too. He who has courage and faith will never perish in misery."

It would be hard to find a more meaningful, inspirational life than the short, very hard life of Anne Frank.

WOULD YOUR DIARY, YOUR

DAILY LIFE, INSPIRE OR

ENCOURAGE SOMEONE ELSE?

ACTION

Take control of your life by taking prompt, positive ACTION toward your objectives. Decide what you should do and do it; make a difference!

YOU DON'T HAVE
TO BE GREAT

to get going, but you do have

to get going to be great.

LES BROWN,
author, speaker

IF YOU WAIT FOR PERFECT CONDITIONS,

I, _____,

WILL TAKE ACTION AND WILL

MAKE A DIFFERENCE.

YOU WILL NEVER GET ANYTHING DONE.

Ecclesiastes 11:4

22

There is an often-told story about a young boy walking on a beach with his grandfather. The beach is littered with starfish that have been washed ashore, stranded there by the receding waves.

The grandfather walks along in silence as the boy bends over again and again to toss the dying starfish back into the water. Finally, the grandfather can hold his tongue no longer. "My boy," he says, "you are

going to exhaust yourself. This beach goes on for miles, and there are so many starfish that you cannot possibly make a difference."

The boy pauses for a moment. He looks at the starfish in his hand and then back at his grandfather. "I'll make a difference to this one," he says, as he throws the starfish into the surf.

In the years to come, you will be given many opportunities to make meaningful differences for yourself and for others if you have the courage to do what you know is right. Act decisively, for those actions will bring many rewards. They will not only help others, but they will also help you believe in yourself.

YOU CAN MAKE

A DIFFERENCE!

QUALITY

QUALITY MEANS BEING THE
BEST YOU THAT YOU CAN BE.
THINKING THE BEST THOUGHTS,
DREAMING THE BEST DREAMS,
DOING YOUR BEST FOR GOD,
FOR YOURSELF, AND FOR OTHERS.

26

YOU DON'T GET
WHAT YOU WANT IN LIFE;

you get what you are.

LES BROWN,
author, speaker

TO THOSE WHO USE WELL WHAT THEY ARE GIVEN,
WILL BE GIVEN, AND THEY WILL HAVE AN ABUNDANCE.
WHO ARE UNFAITHFUL, EVEN WHAT LITTLE

I, _____,

CONSISTENTLY DO MY BEST IN

BIG THINGS OR SMALL, BECAUSE

IT ALL EVENTUALLY ADDS UP

TO WHAT I AM.

EVEN MORE
BUT FROM THOSE
THEY HAVE WILL BE TAKEN AWAY.

Matthew 25:29

28

Les Brown came from inauspicious beginnings. Abandoned as an infant
(although adopted by a wonderful woman), he did not seem to thrive.
He was labeled mentally retarded at his school and therefore was
systematically denied all but the most rudimentary education.
A break came when a caring teacher encouraged Les to refuse the
retarded label and define some goals for himself. So began a
difficult road to building his self-esteem.

Les Brown decided that he wanted to become a radio personality, so
every day he sat in his room, hour after hour, month after month,
listening to the radio and practicing the skills he would need.

When he gained a little confidence, Les tried to get any sort of
job at the local radio station. He was refused and rejected time
and again, but he continued to practice; he returned day after day

until finally he was hired to run errands and empty the trash. He learned everything about the station he could and continued to practice radio skills every day.

At last, his opportunity came. No deejay was available, and Les was the only person in the studio. He got permission to take over until a replacement arrived.

The rest is history. Les Brown went on the air with one of the most commanding and compelling radio voices the industry has ever known.

THE QUALITY OF HIS EFFORTS AS A TEENAGER OPENED THE DOORS FOR AN ENORMOUSLY SUCCESSFUL LIFE.

BELIEF

WHEN YOU BELIEVE IN GOD, IN YOURSELF,
AND IN YOUR DREAMS, YOU WILL ACT WITH
CONVICTION; YOU WILL FIND A WAY TO
OVERCOME EVERY OBSTACLE.

I DON'T WANT
THEM TO FORGET

about [Babe] Ruth; I just want

them to remember me.

HANK AARON,
athlete

COMMIT YOUR WORK TO THE LORD,

I, _____,

AM PASSIONATE ABOUT MY

BELIEFS. I AM TRUE TO GOD,

TO MYSELF, AND TO MY DREAMS—

AND IT SHOWS!

AND THEN YOUR PLANS WILL SUCCEED.

Proverbs 16:3

Hank Aaron faced major challenges: First, he was an African-American who began playing baseball in 1957, when the world of baseball was entirely white and not very open-minded. Second, his coaches spent most of their time trying to correct his faults. They said that he held the bat wrong, that he was impatient at the plate, and that he hit from the wrong foot. They said that he ran the bases wrong, had a hitch in his swing, and didn't get his body into the ball.

But Hank Aaron did not give up, and, in the course of his career, he won practically every honor in baseball, including his dream of breaking Babe Ruth's home-run record. He had great opposition, but he trusted in God and believed in himself and in his dreams, and it paid off!

Everyone who has ever accomplished anything extraordinary had faith enough to take the next step toward the goal, in spite of what others may have said.

TRUST GOD, BELIEVE IN YOURSELF

AND YOUR DREAMS . . .

MAKE THEM COME TRUE!

! ENTHUSIASM

Guess what *ENTHUSIASM* means:
"God in you," or "to be
inspired by God"!

38

NOTHING GREAT WAS EVER ACHIEVED WITHOUT ENTHUSIASM.

RALPH WALDO EMERSON,
American essayist, philosopher

DO THE WILL OF GOD WITH ALL YOUR HEART.
WORK WITH ENTHUSIASM, AS THOUGH
WORKING FOR THE

I, _____,

AM AN ENERGETIC, ENTHUSIASTIC

PERSON!

YOU WERE
LORD RATHER THAN FOR PEOPLE.

Ephesians 6:6-7

Joe Montana has often been described (even by the legendary Joe
Namath) as the best quarterback in football history. Montana played
in four Super Bowl games winning the distinction of Most Valuable
Player in three and was also the NFL MVP in 1989. He once said,
"I've always felt that within myself, I can find a way to win."

Perhaps Joe Montana's greatest strength as a player came from this determination to never give up, no matter how far behind his team happened to be. In fact, many times he almost single-handedly brought his team from far behind to surprising wins. His coaches, his fans, and his teammates all acquired faith in his unwavering enthusiasm for victory. They nicknamed him the Comeback Kid.

What nickname would you like your friends or teammates to assign to you?

IT'S YOUR CHOICE;
MAKE IT A GOOD ONE!

CHARACTER

CHARACTER DOES NOT RESULT
FROM NEVER HAVING MADE A MISTAKE.
(EVERYONE MAKES MISTAKES.) CHARACTER
RESULTS FROM LEARNING FROM
MISTAKES, ASKING FOR FORGIVENESS,
ACCEPTING THE GRACE THAT COMES
WITH FORGIVENESS, AND THEN, HAVING
LEARNED, DOING BETTER THE NEXT TIME.

44

SOW A THOUGHT, REAP AN ACT;

sow an act, reap a habit;

sow a habit, reap a character.

Sow a character; reap a destiny.

ANONYMOUS

THEN YOU WILL UNDERSTAND WHAT IS RIGHT, JUST, AND
OF ACTION EVERY TIME. FOR WISDOM WILL ENTER
JOY. WISE PLANNING WILL WATCH OVER YOU.

I, _____,

SEEK HONORABLE CHARACTER IN

MYSELF AND IN OTHERS.

FAIR, AND YOU WILL KNOW HOW TO FIND THE RIGHT COURSE

YOUR HEART, AND KNOWLEDGE WILL FILL YOU WITH

UNDERSTANDING WILL KEEP YOU SAFE.

Proverbs 2:9–11

One of the nicest and most interesting people I have ever known is astronaut Buzz Aldrin. One afternoon while scuba diving in the Cayman Islands, we were contemplating the incredible clarity of the Caribbean waters as we looked out over the wall where the depth plummeted from seventy feet to over five thousand feet. I told Buzz that sometimes diving the wall made me wonder what it would be like to be an explorer in space. Looking down into the crystal water, so beautiful and blue and enticing on the surface yet so dark and dangerous far below, I asked him a question. "On your trip to the moon, were you aware of a specific point at which blue sky ended and black outer space began?"

He said yes, that there was such a point but that he couldn't see it until he got there.

Many of the decisions that shape character are like that. They are difficult to make in advance. But if you are eager to please God, when you face a decision you will be able to discern the specific point between right and wrong, the specific point between safety and danger, the specific place where the clear blue sky ends and darkness begins.

Sometimes you may be traveling fast when you reach that point. Often there will be tremendous temptation to go on just a little further. Stop and go back to safety.

GO BACK TO A PLACE WHERE YOUR
CHARACTER WILL NOT BE DAMAGED AND
YOUR DESTINY WILL NOT BE COMPROMISED.

VOICE

THE POWER OF ONE VOICE CAN CHANGE MANY THINGS.

USE YOUR VOICE TO SPEAK OUT FOR WHAT IS RIGHT.

IF I EVER GET A CHANCE TO HIT THAT— I'LL HIT IT HARD.

ABRAHAM LINCOLN as a teen,
upon seeing a slave auction

A PERSON'S WORDS CAN BE LIFE-GIVING WATER;
WORDS OF TRUE WISDOM

I, _____,

SPEAK OUT STRONGLY FOR WHAT

I BELIEVE.

ARE AS REFRESHING AS A BUBBLING BROOK.

Proverbs 18:4

The scene was a large auditorium in a city in the South. A huge television screen dominated the room filled with nearly a thousand spectators (mostly men) who had come to watch a remote broadcast of the World Heavyweight Championship bout between an African-American champion and a white contender. The crowd was almost evenly divided between the races and reflected support for each man. The atmosphere was strained, unnaturally quiet. Emotions ran high for this fight. The tension, as they say, could be cut with a knife.

Just before the fight was to begin, a light illuminated the American flag, and the strains of the national anthem began pouring out of the large speakers. No one moved through the first few bars, and it looked as if no one was going to move, when suddenly a young woman stood up and began singing: "What so proudly we hail, at the twilight's last gleaming."

Her chin trembled. She was obviously apprehensive, but she looked
straight ahead, and her voice didn't waver.

A big, burly African-American man stood next. Then, one by one, in
various parts of the audience, men stood to their feet, singing. By
the time the anthem was over, everyone was standing not as whites or
blacks but as Americans. The mood of the entire gathering was changed.

Did you perhaps wonder about the young woman who stood? What was
her name? Was she black or white? It absolutely does not matter.

IT COULD HAVE BEEN YOU.

YOUR VOICE CAN MAKE

A DIFFERENCE.

HERO

Choose a person you respect and admire to be your HERO and learn everything you can from that person. Repeat this again and again all through your life. Find these HEROES in your family. Find them in public life or in books. Find them wherever you can—just find them. Learn their secrets of success. Learn the building blocks of their character. Learn from their mistakes. The life experiences of those you admire can take you further than you could ever go alone. Their influences can guide you down right paths.

TRUE HEROISM IS
REMARKABLY SOBER,

very undramatic. It is not the urge to

surpass all others at whatever cost but the

urge to serve others at whatever cost.

ARTHUR ASHE,
athlete, humanitarian

WHOEVER WALKS WITH THE WISE WILL

WHOEVER WALKS WITH

I, _____,

LEARN FROM THE EXAMPLES

OF MY HEROES.

BECOME WISE;
FOOLS WILL SUFFER HARM.

Proverbs 13:20

Arthur Ashe, an outstanding athlete and humanitarian, died in 1993.
He had contracted the AIDS virus from a blood transfusion following
heart surgery. Arthur wanted to live to see his young daughter
Camera go to dances, enter college, and marry . . . but he did not
live long enough.

Just before he died, he finished his last book, <u>Days of Grace</u>. The
final chapter is a letter to Camera, imploring her to continue to
look to his example and his love for guidance and inspiration.
"Don't be angry with me if I am not there in person, alive and

well, when you need me," he wrote. "I would like nothing more. When you feel sick at heart and weary of life, or when you stumble and fall and don't know if you can get up again, think of me. I will be watching and smiling and cheering you on."

Who are your heroes? Are they leading you where you really want to go?

ARE THEY CHEERING YOU
ON TO GREAT THINGS
IN YOUR LIFE?

LOVE

True LOVE is not a warm, fuzzy feeling. It is not an exciting infatuation. True LOVE is a commitment, a willingness to sacrifice whatever may be necessary for the well-being of the beloved.

THE GREATEST LOVE IS SHOWN

when people lay down their

lives for their friends.

JESUS CHRIST
(in John 15:13)

LOVE IS PATIENT AND KIND. LOVE IS NOT JEALOUS
OR BOASTFUL OR PROUD OR RUDE. LOVE DOES
DEMAND ITS OWN WAY. LOVE IS NOT IRRITABLE, AND IT
IT IS NEVER GLAD ABOUT INJUSTICE BUT REJOICES
NEVER LOSES FAITH, IS ALWAYS HOPEFUL, AND ENDURES

I, _____,

WILL LOVE OTHERS.

NOT

KEEPS NO RECORD OF WHEN IT HAS BEEN WRONGED.

WHENEVER THE TRUTH WINS OUT. LOVE NEVER GIVES UP,

THROUGH EVERY CIRCUMSTANCE. LOVE WILL LAST FOREVER.

1 Corinthians 13:4-8

64

After going through a battery of tests, an eight-year-old boy was asked by his family doctor if he would give his younger sister a blood transfusion that would hopefully save her life. She was critically ill with a disease from which he had recovered and for which he had developed antibodies.

The little boy considered the request for a few moments, and then he quietly agreed. He was subdued as the needle was inserted into his vein and his blood taken; but the physician and his parents were so focused on the seriously ill little sister in the next room that they paid little attention to his solemn mood.

Later, as the transfusion was completed, the boy called the doctor in to ask him a question. When the doctor heard the child's question, he wept. The eight-year-old boy wanted to know if he would have time to say good-bye to his family, or if he would die right away. Not understanding that the procedure was relatively harmless, the little boy believed that in giving his sister his blood, he was giving up his own life to save hers. He had been willing to die for her, to give up everything, because he loved her.

THIS IS A GOOD STORY TO
REMEMBER WHEN PEOPLE TALK
TOO EASILY ABOUT LOVE.

GENEROSITY

IT IS A STRANGE AND WONDERFUL TRUTH
THAT NO MATTER HOW GENEROUS YOU ARE IN
THIS LIFE, YOU WILL ALWAYS GET BACK
MORE THAN YOU GIVE AWAY.

WHEN YOU HAVE GIVEN NOTHING, ASK FOR NOTHING.

ALBANIAN PROVERB

IF YOU GIVE, YOU WILL RECEIVE. YOUR GIFT WILL
PRESSED DOWN, SHAKEN TOGETHER TO MAKE ROOM FOR MORE,
YOU USE IN GIVING—LARGE OR SMALL—IT WILL

I, _____,

AM A GENEROUS,

GIVING PERSON.

RETURN TO YOU IN FULL MEASURE,
AND RUNNING OVER. WHATEVER MEASURE
BE USED TO MEASURE WHAT IS GIVEN BACK TO YOU.

Luke 6:38

GENEROSITY

70

In Philadelphia many years ago, an elderly couple arrived after midnight at the front desk of a third-class hotel in search of a room. Exhausted, they explained that they had found no rooms in any hotel in the city because of a convention. They implored the young desk clerk to not turn them away. The young man hesitated, but, moved by sympathy, he decided to offer the older couple his own room. He apologized that while it was not as nice as one of the regular rental rooms, at least he could make it available for them free since he would be working through the night.

The next morning the couple invited the young man to join them for breakfast. When he arrived, the couple thanked him again for his generosity and told him that he was much too fine a hotel man to be working where he was.

The couple then introduced themselves as Mr. and Mrs. John Jacob Astor. They told him they were planning to build a hotel in New York City and had decided to offer him the top management position.

The hotel they built was the Waldorf-Astoria Hotel, one of the finest in the entire world. The young man became one of the most important hotel men in the world . . . because he was generous enough to give his own room to a tired, elderly couple.

ARE YOU A GIVER?

RESPONSIBILITY

Taking RESPONSIBILITY for your own actions is a good sign that you are growing up. That especially means not blaming someone else for the mistakes that you make.

P.S. *EVERYONE* makes mistakes!

74

DON'T BE AFRAID

to make a mistake.

You can't make anything

if you can't make a mistake.

MARVA COLLINS,
educator

PEOPLE WHO ACCEPT CORRECTION ARE ON THE PATHWAY
BUT THOSE WHO IGNORE IT WILL

I, _____,

AM RESPONSIBLE FOR ME.

TO LIFE,

LEAD OTHERS ASTRAY.

Proverbs 10:17

Marva Collins is one of the most respected educators of this century. She has earned that distinction through many accomplishments in her field. For example, she teaches inner-city elementary children in Chicago a level of academics not often achieved on a junior college level. How do fourth graders read and understand Shakespeare? How do they learn a range of vocabulary words that far exceeds that of their families, indeed, many of their teachers? They are inspired by a woman who loves them and believes in them and who does not hesitate to tell it like it is.

Marva Collins says, "Black America has been led to believe that we are supposed to fail. When we do fail, people look down on us, and that leads to a lot of hate. Things do not have to be that way. We can make them better. You were not born to fail. You were born to succeed. You were born to be millionaires! But you are going to have to learn. No one owes you a thing in this life. I don't want anyone to give you children anything except your dignity."

Just as Marva Collins says to her students, remember that you were born to succeed. You were born to be millionaires. But you are going to have to learn. And you are going to have to take responsibility for your own future.

NO ONE ELSE CAN

DO THAT FOR YOU.

NO!

Chastity sounds like an old-fashioned word. *Self-discipline* and *abstinence* do, too. What about *abortion, addiction, date rape, AIDS, HIV, abuse, pornography, pregnancy, runaway, depression, suicide?* You hear those words and phrases every day, don't you? Don't they scare you?

THE THIEF'S
PURPOSE IS TO STEAL

and kill and destroy. My purpose is to

give life in all its fullness.

JESUS CHRIST
(in John 10:10)

ABOVE ALL ELSE, GUARD YOUR HEART,
EVERYTHING YOU DO. LOOK STRAIGHT AHEAD, AND
DON'T GET SIDETRACKED;

I, _____,

HAVE THE COURAGE AND

SELF-RESPECT TO SAY NO

WHEN IT'S APPROPRIATE.

FOR IT AFFECTS

FIX YOUR EYES ON WHAT LIES BEFORE YOU.

KEEP YOUR FEET FROM FOLLOWING EVIL.

Proverbs 4:23, 25, 27

God didn't make his rules to restrict you; he made them to give you
freedom and an abundant life! God has good reasons for his rules,
but sometimes, in the emotion of a moment, his reasons are
difficult to understand. For example, to a child who is taught not
to play in the street, the street looks like an ideal place to
play, like fun, like freedom. But his very life is at risk there.

Unfortunately, society today does not do a good job of teaching the
dangers of sex outside marriage, of alcohol and drugs, or of
homosexuality and the occult. Instead, movies, music, television,
and peer pressure constantly send opposite messages.

Being influenced by any of these dangers could be the first step toward doing something that you know in your heart is not right. Something that is certainly not God's best for you. Something that is a step off the sidewalk into the street.

When you are tempted (and you will be), consider your choices carefully, because much may be at risk. Respect yourself enough to say no to anything or anybody that would hurt you or someone else. It is worth the effort. . . . You have a wonderful future awaiting you!

YOU ARE A TREASURE FAR
TOO VALUABLE TO BE LOST.

UNDERSTANDING

A Native American proverb says that to UNDERSTAND a man, you have to walk a mile in his moccasins.

As much as possible, try to know others. You will learn compassion, which is the beginning of love, which is the beginning of life.

TO EASE ANOTHER'S HEARTACHE IS TO FORGET ONE'S OWN.

ABRAHAM LINCOLN

FOR I WAS HUNGRY, AND YOU FED ME. I WAS THIRSTY, AND YOU GAVE ME A DRINK. I WAS A STRANGER, AND YOU I WAS NAKED, AND YOU GAVE ME CLOTHING. I WAS SICK, VISITED ME. . . . I ASSURE YOU, WHEN YOU DID IT TO ONE

I, _____,

HAVE COMPASSION AND

UNDERSTANDING FOR OTHERS.

INVITED ME INTO YOUR HOME.

AND YOU CARED FOR ME. I WAS IN PRISON, AND YOU

OF THE LEAST OF THESE . . . YOU WERE DOING IT TO ME!

Matthew 25:35-36, 40

"I am tired of fighting. Our chiefs are killed. . . . The old men are killed. . . . It is cold, and we have no blankets. The little children are freezing to death. My people, some of them, have run away to the hills, and no one knows where they are, perhaps freezing to death. I want time to look for my children and see how many of them I can find. Maybe I shall find them among the dead. Hear me, my chiefs. I am tired; my heart is sick and sad. I will fight no more forever."

Close your eyes and try to imagine what Chief Joseph and his Native American people must have been feeling when he made these famous remarks in 1877.

Now open your eyes and look around your school, your church, your

community. In this melting pot of American society today, there are

people near you whose families have experienced conditions similar

to those described above. Whether they are victims of a war in the

Middle East or a flood in the Midwest, whether they are struggling

with the effects of a disaster or a disease, this world is a hard

place for a lot of people.

Do you have understanding and compassion for their suffering?

CAN YOU NOT ONLY COUNT YOUR
BLESSINGS BUT SHARE THEM
WITH THOSE LESS FORTUNATE?

MANNERS

Sincere good MANNERS will take you far. Good MANNERS are a measuring stick of both self-worth and respect for others. Having good MANNERS means that you are thoughtful, helpful, and considerate to those around you. Almost any situation can be handled in a mannerly fashion.

IF THIS IS COFFEE, PLEASE BRING ME SOME TEA;

but if this is tea, please bring me some coffee.

ABRAHAM LINCOLN

BUT WHEN THE HOLY SPIRIT CONTROLS OUR LIVES, HE
LOVE, JOY, PEACE, PATIENCE, KINDNESS,

I, _____,

WILL PRACTICE GOOD MANNERS.

WILL PRODUCE THIS KIND OF FRUIT IN US:
GOODNESS, FAITHFULNESS, GENTLENESS, AND SELF-CONTROL.

Galatians 5:22-23

A thoughtful, considerate, and helpful person can be assured of a welcome in almost any group; however, a person who is rude and self-absorbed is rarely received with anything beyond pained tolerance.

Never let yourself be impressed or intimidated by those who swagger about, blowing their own horns, stepping on toes. Anyone with this great need to build himself up at the expense of others is only to be pitied and is certainly not worthy of emulation.

Instead, imitate those who are willing to extend themselves in order to make others more comfortable, especially those who are considerate of friend and stranger alike. Remember, true good manners do not depend on what might be given in return, but on the self-worth of the giver. The Bible says, "If you think you are too important to help someone in need, you are only fooling yourself" (Galatians 6:3).

THE STRONGEST AND BEST PEOPLE ALWAYS HAVE TIME TO BE CONSIDERATE AND SENSITIVE TO THOSE AROUND THEM.

YES!

By saying an enthusiastic YES to the things of God, you are automatically saying no to the evil and the mediocre of this world.

IN ORDER TO LEAD

the orchestra, you have to turn

your back on the crowd.

HEARTLAND SAMPLERS

WHOEVER PURSUES GODLINESS AND UNFAILING LOVE WILL

I, _____,

SAY YES TO THE THINGS

OF GOD!

FIND LIFE, GODLINESS AND HONOR.

Proverbs 21:21

In an exercise to memorize Scripture, Jeneanne "Nini" Sieck copied
her favorite Bible verses onto small cards, which she then
decorated, laminated, and fastened together with rings. She created
the first of what was to become widely known as a perpetual
calendar. After hand-lettering a few of these for her friends and
family, she began photocopying her work and, with her three young

sons as collators, making these little books of Scripture available for sale at craft shows and local shops. The time was the early eighties, and she was a housewife.

Within seven years, Nini's business, Heartland Samplers, was spread around the world. Her product line had expanded to include dozens of items, and her first calendar, <u>Bless Your Heart,</u> had sold more than 2,500,000 copies. All because a housewife disciplined herself to memorize Scripture.

Nini Sieck's success is an example of the success that comes from putting God first in your life.

ISN'T IT EXCITING TO

IMAGINE WHAT GOD HAS

IN STORE FOR YOU?

103

INSPIRATION

INSPIRATION IS A MESSAGE FROM GOD'S HEART TO YOUR HEART. LEARN TO LISTEN CAREFULLY, BECAUSE INSPIRATION IS THE SOURCE OF YOUR DREAMS.

104

SOMETIMES GOD PUSHES US TO WHAT WE HAVE NEVER TRIED.

Sometimes it is uncomfortable to break

the norm. However, when we are

obedient to his requests, . . . in spite

of all the odds, we win.

PHIL DRISCOLL,
composer, performer

NOW GLORY BE TO GOD! BY HIS MIGHTY POWER AT WORK
HE IS ABLE TO ACCOMPLISH INFINITELY MORE THAN

IN ALL MY WAYS

I, _____,

ACKNOWLEDGE GOD,

AND HE DIRECTS MY PATHS.

WITHIN US,

WE WOULD EVER DARE TO ASK OR HOPE.

Ephesians 3:20

As a young California minister with a big dream for a big church but no funds to acquire a church building, Robert Schuller was inspired to begin preaching each Sunday at a drive-in movie theater. As you might imagine, he was laughed at and criticized by many of his peers in the ministry. He was certainly laughed at by the public at large.

His congregation didn't laugh, however. Many of them had never attended a conventional church, and many who had attended one had still never heard the simple good news that God loved them and wanted only the best for them. This good news was so exciting and so well received that Robert Schuller's congregation grew and grew and grew.

Today, in Garden Grove, California, the magnificent Crystal
Cathedral has replaced the drive-in theater. Robert Schuller has
written several books, and his sermons are broadcast around the
world. What a blessing for millions that this young minister
listened to the inspiration of God rather than to the criticism of
his peers.

DO YOU THINK GOD IS
SPEAKING TO YOUR HEART
ABOUT A BIG DREAM?

TRUTH

THE GREATEST LIE IS THAT A SMALL LIE IS HARMLESS. EVERY EVIL THE WORLD HAS KNOWN BEGAN WITH A SMALL LIE.

TRUTH IS AS OLD AS GOD.

EMILY DICKINSON,
American poet

UNLESS YOU ARE FAITHFUL IN SMALL MATTERS, YOU WON'T
EVEN A LITTLE, YOU WON'T BE HONEST WITH GREATER

I, _____,

WILL TELL THE TRUTH.

BE FAITHFUL IN LARGE ONES. IF YOU CHEAT
RESPONSIBILITIES.

Luke 16:10

112

Everyone knows the story of the boy who cried wolf. He got eaten. An extreme example of the consequences of lying or is it? What about a young man who helps himself to a twenty-dollar bill from his mom's purse without permission, or a young woman who lies to her parents about a date that is off-limits? Pretty small stuff, you might think.

But the truth is, unless he sees the error of his ways, that young man is apt to steal again and again. Perhaps later, he will steal a car or rob a business. And if that young woman doesn't change, she will continue to lie to her parents and soon find herself in all sorts of painful situations. Finally, if things go unchecked, their

scenarios will read like soap-opera scripts filled with pain and
betrayal, crime and punishment, and perhaps even divorce, adultery,
or death.

Being dishonest is a trap. It always starts with seemingly minor
things: cheating a little in school, lying to a coach, helping
yourself to a small something that is not yours. But,
unfortunately, if left unchecked, dishonesty grows and grows.

If there is any dishonesty in your life, get rid of it now, before
the roots get any deeper.

ASK GOD; HE WILL HELP.

KINDNESS

THERE IS NEVER A GOOD ENOUGH REASON
NOT TO BE KIND. YOU NEVER KNOW
WHO IS HAVING A HARD DAY . . .
OR A HARD LIFE.

ALWAYS BE KIND.

Remember, the people you meet are

all fighting their own personal battles;

a great number of them are losing,

and many have already lost.

CELINE

YOUR OWN SOUL IS NOURISHED WHEN YOU ARE KIND; BUT

EVEN WHEN I HAVE GOOD REASON,

EVEN WHEN IT IS MOST DIFFICULT,

I, _____,

RESOLVE TO BE KIND AND

TO FORGIVE.

YOU DESTROY YOURSELF WHEN YOU ARE CRUEL.

Proverbs 11:17

It is usually a pleasure to be kind, to bask in the goodwill that
kindness can bring back to you. But there are times when kindness
must include forgiveness, and forgiveness is always a sacrifice.
In response to rudeness, rejection, or pain, retaliation seems like
a much more satisfying choice than kindness. But this is an area in
which you have to trust God's wisdom.

Corrie ten Boom was a middle-aged woman who lived in Holland during
the Nazi occupation. She and her family hid Jewish people in their
house to save them from the extermination camps. Finally, they were
caught and sent to the camps themselves. Corrie suffered tortures
and indignities more horrible than can be imagined, including
watching her family murdered. Yet she always tried to be kind and
to share the gospel even with her oppressors. This was her
sacrifice of obedience to God.

Years later, after her release, she was teaching in a church in Germany when a former SS officer approached her and asked for her forgiveness. Even though he had come to God since then and was now repentant, Corrie remembered that this particular officer had been the cruelest of all. He had been directly involved in killing her sister. Now he stood waiting for her response with his hand extended.

Corrie said that perhaps the hardest sacrifice she ever made was obeying God and taking the SS officer's hand in hers. But, she said, when she did it, the power of heaven fell on her in such strength that it was the greatest blessing of her entire life!

IS THERE SOMEONE TO WHOM

YOU SHOULD SHOW KINDNESS?

FORGIVENESS?

EXTRA

Give a little EXTRA in everything
you do.
It will come back to you in
many ways: Especially in the person
you will become.

DO WHAT YOU CAN,
WITH WHAT YOU HAVE,
WHERE YOU ARE.

TEDDY ROOSEVELT,
twenty-sixth president of
the United States

IT IS POSSIBLE TO GIVE FREELY AND BECOME MORE
BUT THOSE WHO ARE STINGY WILL LOSE EVERYTHING. THE
THOSE WHO REFRESH OTHERS WILL THEMSELVES

I, _____,

GO THE EXTRA MILE. I TRY TO

GIVE BACK MORE THAN I GET.

WEALTHY,

GENEROUS PROSPER AND ARE SATISFIED;

BE REFRESHED.

Proverbs 11:24-25

Michael Jordan is the king of basketball for one reason. His life

shows a pattern that is always part of a winner's profile:

a willingness to give more than is required. Michael always

practiced more, and he always tried to give back more even before

he enjoyed the success he has today. For years, he would stop in

the same tough neighborhood after games and just hang out with the

kids. He wanted them to know that they were important, that

somebody cared about them.

Michael was not always the self-assured person we see now. As a

teen he was so self-conscious about having big ears that he thought

he would never be able to find a wife. He even signed up for a
class in home economics to learn to sew and cook for himself!

He has been rejected, and he has made some mistakes. He was cut
from his high school varsity team and then suspended from school
for skipping classes to practice basketball. He suffered tragedy
when his father was murdered at the height of his fame. Any of
these things, self-consciousness, rejection, or grief, might have
caused a less committed person to give up. But Michael Jordan did
not. The rest is history. He continues to go the extra mile.
Remember, you are responsible for your history, too.

IT'S UP TO YOU!

FRIENDSHIP

FRIENDSHIP MEANS TO TREAT OTHERS IN A WAY THAT THEY CAN ALWAYS TRUST YOU—WITH THEIR POSSESSIONS, WITH THEIR FEELINGS, AND ESPECIALLY WITH THEIR CONFIDENCES— THROUGH GOOD TIMES AND BAD.

BE COURTEOUS TO ALL BUT
CLOSE WITH FEW, and let those few be
well tried before you give them your confidence.
True friendship is a plant of slow growth and
must suffer and withstand the shocks of
hardship before it is entitled to the name.

GEORGE WASHINGTON

THERE ARE "FRIENDS" WHO DESTROY
BUT A REAL FRIEND

I, _____,

AM A LOYAL AND TRUSTWORTHY

FRIEND.

EACH OTHER,
STICKS CLOSER THAN A BROTHER.

Proverbs 18:24

History is filled with accounts of friendships and alliances that have changed not only the courses of individual lives but the affairs of nations. Many of the friendships you make now will have great bearing on what you will become as an adult. As good food will nourish your body, good friends will nourish your soul.

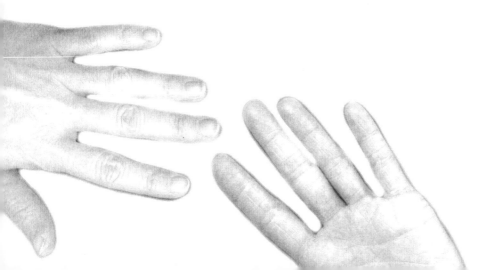

There is someone in your neighborhood or your class or your church who would like you for a friend. Look for that person beyond the limits of age or race, and especially don't worry about who might be the most popular. Look beneath the surface for the glimmer of good character; look for someone who will help you bring out the best in yourself. Finding a friend like that is like finding a treasure.

The Bible says that one can put a thousand to flight, but two can put ten thousand to flight.

INVEST YOURSELF IN FRIENDSHIPS
THAT CAN HELP CHANGE THE WORLD.

PERSEVERANCE

GREAT THINGS ARE ACHIEVED IN
LIFE BY THOSE WHO ACQUIRE THE HABIT
OF PRACTICING PERSEVERANCE. AND
IT TAKES JUST THAT—PRACTICING.

NEVER QUIT.

Never, never, never, never quit.

Never quit!

WINSTON CHURCHILL,
British prime minister during
World War II

SO DON'T GET TIRED OF DOING WHAT
FOR WE WILL REAP A HARVEST

I, _____,

DO NOT QUIT. I PERSEVERE!

IS GOOD . . . AND GIVE UP,
OF BLESSINGS AT THE APPROPRIATE TIME.

Galatians 6:9

Aileen, a gifted newborn and obstetrical nurse at Columbia
Presbyterian Hospital in New York City, tells the following story
about perseverance.

"When my own baby was born, I found myself spending hours on end
leaning on the window of the hospital nursery, watching not only
the newborns but the nurses who were caring for them. I could
hardly believe that people could actually be paid money for doing
something as joyful and fulfilling as helping bring these little
ones into the world.

"That night I told my husband, John, how I'd love to be a nurse.
He said that I should; but, of course, I knew it was impossible.
We had no money, and no one in my family had ever gone to college.
I knew that I was not college material either. I put the thought
away and began raising my family.

"However, through many hard years, John didn't forget. Every month he put a little something aside. One day, he came to me with a sum of money that he had saved so I could go to college and become a nurse.

"At first I couldn't believe it. Then, because I had so little self-esteem, I refused. I explained to him that I could never pass college that I would only fail and embarrass us. But he persevered. He convinced me to take just one course.

"I made an A+ in that freshman English course, and the rest is history. Here I am today a nurse at one of the finest hospitals in the world. All because my husband persevered. All because he wouldn't quit."

ALL BECAUSE HE NEVER
STOPPED BELIEVING IN ME.

WORK

No worthwhile dream was ever achieved without WORK, and a lot of it. But a well-kept secret is that WORK can be more enjoyable and more exciting than almost anything. WORKING toward a dream is like taking a journey. You will enjoy getting there if you are sure that your destination is where you really want to go.

I AM ONLY AN AVERAGE MAN,

but I work harder at it than the average man.

THOMAS JEFFERSON,
third president of the
United States

THOSE WHO WORK HARD WILL PROSPER

I, _____,

AM A HARD AND WILLING WORKER.

AND BE SATISFIED.

Proverbs 13:4

Many years ago, a wealthy and influential European merchant named

Rothschild decided to do business in America. He called three of

his employees separately and asked each one how soon each could set

sail to San Francisco and begin the work. The first man gave the

question considerable thought and finally answered that he would do

his best to be ready in ten days. The second man assured Rothschild

that he would need only three days to get ready. The third man

answered immediately, "I am ready at once."

"Good," said Rothschild to the third man. "From today on you are a partner in our new firm in San Francisco, and you will sail tomorrow."

That third man was Julius May, who became one of San Francisco's and America's richest and most influential men. Julius May's willingness to work was the beginning of his success.

What about you? Are you willing to start working for what you want?

ARE YOU READY TO SUCCEED?

SUCCESS

There are almost as many definitions of success as there are successful people, but my favorite is a quote from international businessman, former sportscaster and Miami Dolphins football player Tim Foley. Tim says that "Success is a journey . . . not a destination."

IN MOST THINGS, YOU FAIL YOUR WAY TO SUCCESS.

So failing is more than just OK; it's part of the

experience you need to get you to the top.

TY BOYD,
speaker, author

COMMIT EVERYTHING YOU DO
TO THE LORD. TRUST

I, _____,

HAVE EVERYTHING IT TAKES TO

BECOME A SUCCESSFUL PERSON!

HIM, AND HE WILL HELP YOU.

Psalm 37:5

Jim Tunney, an outstanding figure in the worlds of both education and sports, tells the following story about the California Special Olympics, illustrating that a success that might seem nothing to one person might mean everything to his neighbor—the journey is what matters.

"I was standing about twenty feet from the victory stand when a 26-year-old mentally, physically and emotionally challenged man received his award for winning the 100-meter dash. As the judge placed the gold medal around his neck, the young man simply said, 'Thanks.'

"I looked at his sponsor, who was standing next to me. Tears began rolling down her cheeks.

"'That's a marvelous accomplishment for that young man,' I said.

"The sponsor continued crying as she answered me.'Yes, it is,' she said. 'That's the first word that young man has ever spoken in his life.'"

REMEMBER, SUCCESS IS A JOURNEY, NOT A DESTINATION.

A FINAL NOTE

It is my prayer that you will find the courage and inspiration to seek God's will at the turning points in your life, because there you will find joy and abundance and peace. There you will find your greatest dreams fulfilled. God bless you on your journey.

C. W. M.